$\mathcal{B}e$ CALM

*31 Mindful Affirmations
and Reflections for Living
a Peaceful Life*

YVELETTE STINES

*31 Mindful Affirmations
and Reflections for Living
a Peaceful Life*

Yvelette Stines

Be Calm: 31 Mindful Affirmations and
Reflections for Living a Peaceful Life

Copyright © 2016 by Yvelette Stines
ISBN: 978-0-9849990-2-6

All rights reserved. Published by Calming Corners
No part of this publication may be stored in a retrieval system, transmitted in any form or reproduced by any means: electronic, mechanical, photocopying, recording, or otherwise without written permission from the publisher, author, and illustrators.

Author: Yvelette Stines
Editor: Bettina Ortez
Designer: LaTanya Orr

Printed in The United States of America

Dedication

This book is dedicated to the people who are working hard to make their dreams come true.

Gratitude

With humility and grace I thank God, my family,
friends, supporters, and ancestors.

*Bettye Stines, Yves Stines, Bettina Ortez,
Ignaciao Ortez, Joshua Ortez, Kinyel Friday,
Niki Johnson, Julie D. Andrews, Dr. Linda Selim,
April Ray, Dr. LeConte Dill, Dr. Elaine Carey,
Elizabeth Whittaker-Walker, Charlena Ponders,
Francina James, Rebecca Rudnicki, Louise Spector*

INTRODUCTION

Welcome to your new journey of living a calm and mindful life. This book is designed to give you doable action steps that will help you mindfully live calm and peaceful.

On each page you will find an action step, quote, reflection, and affirmation that will guide you towards creating a mindful and peaceful life. You can choose a word and reflect on it for a day, a week, or a month. This is your journey. Take your time and be gentle with yourself. Take the word/action step, put it into to practice, meditate on the quotes, read the reflections, take time to journal about your journey, and repeat the affirmations. In the back of the book you will find blank pages for your personal notes and reflections.

Enjoy the book and your new journey of living mindful and peaceful.

Peace and blessings,
Yvelette Stines

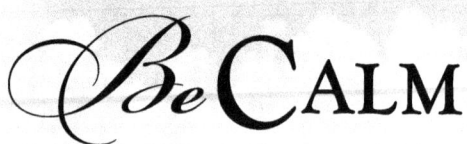

Be CALM

31 Mindful Words for Peaceful Living

1. BREATHE
2. EXERCISE
3. PRAY
4. PAMPER
5. VISUALIZE
6. GRATITUDE
7. LISTEN
8. PREPARE
9. SLEEP
10. NOURISH
11. THINK
12. GIVE
13. FORGIVE
14. RISK
15. SMILE
16. EAT
17. RELEASE
18. CONTINUE
19. LOVE
20. DECIDE
21. FOCUS
22. ORGANIZE
23. PLAY
24. CREATE
25. LAUGH
26. TRUST
27. ENLIGHTEN
28. WRITE
29. MEDITATE
30. REFLECT
31. DREAM

Breathe

"Regulate the breathing, and thereby control the mind." B.K.S. Iyengar

Deep breathing is essential for your health. It releases toxins, calms you down, and helps you become mindful and present. Deep breathing also naturally improves our immune, lymph, and digestive system.

YOUR ACTION STEP:
Practice deep breathing daily.

AFFIRMATION:
My breath gives me an abundance of life.

Exercise

"Exercise should be regarded as tribute to the heart." Gene Tunney

If you want to get focused, happy, healthy, and release some weight, exercise is essential. This is a wonderful way to reduce stress. If you haven't moved in a while give yourself 30 minutes two times a week and add on from there. You will feel so good it will become a habit. Make the time and show up for yourself.

Your Action Step:
Schedule time to exercise and commit to it. You owe it to yourself.

Affirmation:
When I exercise, I am strengthening my mind, body, and soul.

"Prayer is simply talking to God like a friend and should be the easiest thing we do each day." Joyce Meyer

God hears everything it is all on his timing, your obedience, and when you are ready to receive it. Spend quiet time with your higher source. This time will give you guidance, peace, restoration, and the wisdom and instruction that you need to move forward. There is a plan for your life and all you have to do is ask, be patient, and follow instructions. That soft whisper, at times, can turn into a loud roar. This is your guidance system from your higher source. Some call it spirit, vibes, or intuition. Listen well and follow instruction. Sometimes it doesn't make sense but it all works out.

Your Action Step:
Take time out daily and spend time with your higher source through meditation and prayer.

Affirmation:
I know that everything in my life is working for my highest good.

Pamper

"When you recover or discover something that nourishes your soul and brings joy, care enough about yourself to make room for it in your life." Jean Shinoda Bolen

It is important to pause and take care of yourself. We have so many responsibilities and somehow we forget to schedule ourselves in. Find activities that bring you joy and activities that will allow you to release stress and clear your mind. This is a necessity for survival. Create a habit of practicing self-care.

YOUR ACTION STEP:
Schedule time for yourself daily.

AFFIRMATION:
When I honor and take care of myself, I can effectively take care of others.

Visualize

"What the mind can conceive and believe it can achieve."
Napoleon Hill

Sometimes we are so caught up in our
daily responsibilities that we forget
to create a vision for ourselves. There
are times that we start to create a vision
surrounded by our present circumstance.
Pause, visualize, dream big, dream bigger,
pray, and get to work.

Your Action Step:
Dream big and visualize the
life you want daily.

Affirmation:
My vision is supported by the universe.
I am patient and ready.

Gratitude

"Develop an attitude of gratitude, and give thanks for everything that happens to you, knowing that every step forward is a step toward achieving something bigger and better than your current situation."
Brian Tracey

There is a beautiful thing that happens when we are grateful for what we have. We learn to see the positivity and blessings regardless of the situation. There are times that we complain when things are not going our way. Try to see the positive side and find gratitude in each situation. Your life will change and there will be a natural flow of abundance.

Your Action Step:
For 30 days write down 5- 10 things you are grateful for.

Affirmation:
I am grateful for everything I encounter. There is a lesson and blessing in every situation.

Listen

"Listening is such a simple act. It requires us to be present, and that takes practice, but we don't have to do anything else. We don't have to advise, or coach, or sound wise. We just have to be willing to sit there and listen." Margaret J. Wheatley

There is beauty in the art of closing your mouth and opening your ears. Listen to your intuition, that small voice that eventually gets louder. The hunch that sits at the pit of your stomach. This is your higher source guiding you, this is THE perfect GPS. Learn to listen to others without anticipating what they are going to say or how you are going to reply, be present with your ears open and listen well.

Your Action Step:
Start and sustain a practice of listening with your full presence.

Affirmation:
I am truly present and I put off other thoughts in order to listen.

Prepare

"There is no short cut to achievement. Life requires thorough preparation."
George Washington Carver

You never know when an opportunity will present itself. Always be prepared. We are guided and put through tests to prepare us what we prayed for. Pay attention and stay ready.

Your Action Step:
Consistently prepare yourself for the life you want to live.

Affirmation:
I am spiritually, emotionally, mentally, and physically prepared for my dreams to become my reality.

Sleep

"Sleep is the best meditation."
Dalai Lama

Sleep. It is essential for your health.
It aids in weight loss. It helps you
release stress. It is also a time for your
subconscious mind and intuition
to work through your dreams.

YOUR ACTION STEP:
Make sleep a priority.

AFFIRMATION:
My sleep is essential for my mind,
body, and soul.

"Take Care of Yourself. You have one body and one life."
Yvelette Stines

Your mental, physical, and emotional health are essential and important for your mind, body, and soul. Watch your thoughts, the company you keep, the food you eat, and the conversations that you have, particularly with yourself. Be mindful, present, purposeful, move more for physical activity, and practice a habit of self-care

YOUR ACTION STEP:
Create a health plan. Do something daily or weekly that will improve your well-being.

AFFIRMATION:
Good health is my birth right. I bless my body daily and take good care of it.

Think

"The key to creating the mental space before responding is mindfulness. Mindfulness is a way of being present: paying attention to and accepting what is happening in our lives. It helps us to be aware of and step away from our automatic and habitual reactions to our everyday experiences."
Elizabeth Thornton

Mindfulness is an important element of survival. In any situation think and take some time to think again. Ask yourself the right questions before you act and/or react. Others' actions towards you is not always about you. The key is being unapologetically truthful with yourself. We move quickly at times and don't stop to reflect about the why and our specific intentions. Sometimes we are caught up in our routine we forget about the true meaning of why we are here in the first place. Check in with yourself throughout the day, make sure you are better than okay. Take the time, pay attention, and stay mindful. Mindfulness will help you learn a lot about yourself this is when we can fully understand others.

Your Action Step:
Stop. Think. Ask the right questions. When waiting for the answer pay attention to your body, your surroundings, and thoughts. Stay mindful.

Affirmation:
I make all decisions from a place of mindfulness and truth.

Give

"As we work to create light for others, we naturally light our own way." Mary Anne Radmacher

When you give without expecting
accolades or anything in return, this is
when you are truly giving from your heart.
Being of service and giving to others
is the greatest gift we can receive.

You Action Step:
Give without an intention of
getting anything in return.

Affirmation:
When I give to others, their joy
and happiness is a gift to me.
When I give I receive.

Forgive

"It's one of the greatest gifts you can give yourself, to forgive. Forgive everybody." Maya Angelou

When you forgive you are freeing yourself and releasing the person and situation that caused you pain. Forgiveness is not for them, it is for you. Holding on to grudges will weigh you down, and subconsciously attract the same situation over and over. Leave them be and understand we are a reflection of our actions. Keep your life free, positive, and purposeful.

Your Action Step:
Forgive yourself fully and forgive everything else.

Affirmation:
When I forgive and release fully and completely, I know I am strong, courageous, loving, and free.

Risk

*"Take chances, make mistakes.
That's how you grow. Pain nourishes
your courage. You have to fail in
order to practice being brave."*
Mary Tyler Moore

We have to take that bold chance
that will shift us in the right direction.
It is not supposed to feel calm or
comfortable. The growth comes with
finding comfort in being uncomfortable.
Take the chance with faith and
fearlessness and watch the beauty
and blessings unfold.

Your Action Step:
Take a chance on your dreams.
Make a list of small actions steps
that will help you make your
dreams come true.

Affirmation:
I am brave and open to accept
the positive changes that come
with taking a chance.

Smile

"Let your smile change the world, but don't let the world change your smile." ~Unknown

Your smile could be the one thing that will make someone's day. There are moments that happen that make us smile. Remember those special moments on a daily basis. When your feel like the weight of the world is on your shoulders, take a deep breath, close your eyes, think of something that brings you happiness and just smile.

Your Action Step:
Smile at least 10 times on a daily basis.

Affirmation:
My positive energy and light extends to others through my smile.

"The food you eat can be either the safest and most powerful form of medicine or the slowest form of poison." Ann Wigmore

A healthy outside starts on the inside. The foods that you choose will affect your mind, body, and soul. Try to eat a plant-based diet full of live foods, fresh fruits, and vegetables. Eating clean will help your body naturally get rid of toxins.

Your Action Step:
Keep your plate full of colorful live foods to keep your mind, body, and soul nourished.

Affirmation:
I eat to nourish my body so I can live my best life, protect my legacy, and be an example for others.

Release

"Letting go helps us to live in a more peaceful state of mind and helps restore our balance. It allows others to be responsible for themselves and not for us to take our hands off situations that do not belong to us. This frees us from unnecessary stress." Melody Beattie

When we hold on to things
we are allowing baggage and toxins
to store in our body. Free yourself and
release what no longer serves you.
Understand the lesson, reason,
learn from it and let it go.

Your Action Step:
What are you holding on to?
Pray on it, write about it, and take steps
to let it go so you can grow.

Affirmation:
This is my present moment. I choose
to release the past. My future is an
abundance of freedom and happiness.

Continue

"You simply have to put one foot in front of the other and keep going. Put blinders on and plow right ahead."
George Lucas

The destination to your greatness
is not a straight path. You will fall,
make mistakes, mess up, and question
your initial "why". Whatever you do,
don't give up. Setbacks are stepping
stones for your set up to greatness.
Take a quick break but don't let the
challenge break you. Keep going and
continue until you get what you want.

YOUR ACTION STEP:
Keep going. Don't Stop.
Remember your why.

AFFIRMATION:
I have what it takes. I am more
than enough. I will make it.

Love

"Love makes your soul crawl out from its hiding place." Zora Neale Hurston

Love starts with self. If you don't love your whole self, you can't fully love anyone else. When we spread love, love comes back to us in many ways. When we respond with love, it helps our emotional and mental state. It is not easy to respond with love all the time. I encourage you to remember hurt people hurt people and the individuals who are most difficult to get along with need the most love.

YOUR ACTION STEP:
Respond with love. Spread love. Share love.

AFFIRMATION:
I deeply love and accept myself so I can deeply love and accept others

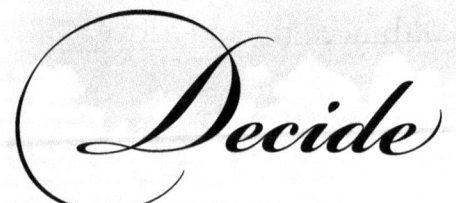

"What you do today can improve all your tomorrows." Ralph Marston

Allow your future self to thank you by making decisive and purposeful decisions today. Make decisions that are aligned with your why, happiness, and led by your higher source. We have to live with ourselves and our decisions. It is okay to take your time, think it through, and listen to your inner guides. Sometimes it won't make sense, but have the faith that it will all work out.

Your Action Step:
Be unapologetically decisive with your decisions. Walk by faith not by sight.

Affirmation:
I am confident that I make the decisions that serve the purpose of my life.

Focus

"Focus on the journey, not the destination. Joy is found not in finishing an activity but in doing it."
Greg Anderson

There is a plan and purpose for your life, you were given the dream, idea, and goal for a reason. It is your job to stay focused and make it a habit. It is important to release the physical, emotional, and spiritual clutter so you can have a focused mind to accomplish greatness. Before you make a decision, think of your aligned purpose and goals.

Your Action Step:
Focus on a task for 30-45 minutes with no distractions. Check in with your why and purpose before you make a decision.

Affirmation:
I am committed to staying present and focused.

"For every minute spent organizing an hour is earned." Benjamin Franklin

When you are organized, your life will flow with ease. There are so many demands with life, being in a constant state of disorganization will leave you mentally cluttered and chaotic. If you have things in order, it is easy to navigate your life, plan ahead, and accomplish a lot more in less time.

YOUR ACTION STEP:
Take one area of your life at a time and put an organizational system in place.

AFFIRMATION:
I owe it to myself to be organized, so I can stay stress free and focused.

"Life must be lived as play." Plato

You should play just as you work.
Life is about being in the moment,
having a good laugh and enjoying the
moments of play. It is important
to have fun in life.

YOUR ACTION STEP:
Enjoy your time on this earth.
Happiness is your birthright.

AFFIRMATION:
I am free to play and enjoy my life.

Create

"Every story I create, creates me.
I write to create myself."
Octavia E. Butler

Art is like a massage for the soul. It awakes our spirit and speaks to places within us of the unknown. It is a blessing to get lost in the power of creativity. Give yourself the time and freedom to create.

YOUR ACTION STEP:
Take time out weekly to do something creative.

AFFIRMATION:
I am a creative being who has a powerful imagination.

"*Laughter is a tranquilizer with no side effects.*" Arnold H. Glasow

Laughter is a gift that brings happiness, memories, and bonds with others. Everyone has a different sense of humor. Reminisce on a time that you heard a laugh so infectious that you started to smile and laugh. Think of the natural laughter from a child and a smile is inevitable.

Your Action Step:
Have a good belly laugh on a regular basis.

Affirmation:
I am ready to unapologetically smile and laugh out loud.

Trust

"All things come when the timing is right. Trust and believe it is when you are ready to receive." Unknown

Understand that we consistently get our needs met, and our wants appear when we are ready. We must trust and have patience that all will come in due time. Every step is preparation for our next steps. Align yourself accordingly, trust, and ask for specific direction.

Your Action Step:
Learn the art of patience and know you are right where you are supposed to be. If you are seeking change. Do something daily for your personal, emotional, spiritual, and physical growth.

Affirmation:
I am patient and I trust myself. I understand my thought creates my reality and I will consciously think positive thoughts.

Enlighten

"True wisdom listens more, talks less and can get along with all types of people." Kiana Tom

We learn from our mistakes and we can learn from others' mistakes. Once we learn, we don't repeat the mistakes; if we do, it is now a choice. We must pay attention, the lessons come in different forms until we fully learn. When we understand that we have the gift of wisdom to teach and guide others, we must honor the gift. Be mindful of the advice and information we share to others, as some are not ready to receive the guidance.

Your Action Step:
Seek wisdom daily and cherish this priceless gift.

Affirmation:
My wisdom keeps me balanced and grounded.

"Whether you're keeping a journal or writing as a meditation, it's the same thing. What's important is you're having a relationship with your mind."
Natalie Goldberg

Journaling is a powerful activity. The art of writing your thoughts and feelings can heal in powerful and deep ways. Intentional journaling or freewriting can reveal many truths and answers that we are seeking.

Your Action Step:
Take time daily or weekly to write. Get your favorite pen and a notebook, set your timer and write freely from your soul.

Affirmation:
I fearlessly share my thoughts on the page as my heart and soul speak to me.

Meditate

"To meditate means to go home to yourself. Then you know how to take care of the things that are happening inside you, and you know how to take care of the things that happen around you." Thich Nhat Hanh

A consistent meditation practice
will improve your life abundantly.
With a daily practice of meditation your
world will improve mentally, physically,
spiritually, and emotionally.

YOUR ACTION STEP:
Meditate daily. Start with five minutes
and gradually add time.

AFFIRMATION:
Meditation enhances my life in
all areas and helps me develop a
divine relationship with myself.

Reflect

"In a mirror is where we find a reflection of our appearances, but in a heart is where we find a reflection of our soul." Ester Escalante

It is essential to take some quality time to reflect. There are things in our past that shape who we are today. Reflection is an important part of our life process. It shows us how far we've come and what we need to do to have a wonderful and purposeful future.

Your Action Step:
Take time to reflect on the past, think about how it has helped your present situation, and how it will enhance your future.

Affirmation:
I am grateful for my past that has led me to this present moment.

"Trust in dreams, for in them is the hidden gate to eternity." *Kahlil Gibran*

God gives us a seed that is within our soul. That is our dream. He supplies us with the natural gifts, this is for us to develop and share it with the world. This seed was placed in you for a reason. It is your job to protect and nurture it with all of your heart. Follow your dreams fearlessly, the path is not straight or easy but is definitely worth it.

Your Action Step:
Do an intentional and purposeful action daily that will help you achieve your dreams.

Affirmation:
When I truly focus on my why and work towards my dreams, I understand everything in my life is preparing me to make my dreams come true.

Be Calm

Reflect and Write on Living a Peaceful Life

Be Calm

Reflect and Write about the Action Step that You are Excited to Implement.

Be Calm: 31 Mindful Affirmations & Reflections for Living a Peaceful Life 69

Be Calm

Reflect and Write about the Action Step that Scares You Most.

Be Calm

Reflect and Write about Three Ways You will Commit to Living a Peaceful Life.

Be Calm

Reflect and write about the first affirmation you will implement.

Be Calm

Reflect and Write about the Quote that Resonated with You most.

Be Calm

Write and Reflect on the First Action Step that You will Incorporate in Your Life.

Be Calm: 31 Mindful Affirmations & Reflections for Living a Peaceful Life

Be Calm

Reflect and Write Fearlessly on the Following Pages.

Be Calm: 31 Mindful Affirmations & Reflections for Living a Peaceful Life

About the Author

Yvelette Stines is an author and educator. She is the founder of **Calming Corners**, a blog and lifestyle brand that motivates people to live a calm life and write from their soul. She has taught many workshops on wellness, healing, and writing. She uses these focus points to help clients and students identify their greatest potential for healing, creativity, and living well. Her work has been published in *Essence, Heart and Soul, The Root, The Source, Jones Magazine, Mind Body Green, Black Enterprise, Green Build + Design*, and more. Stines first book **Vernon the Vegetable Man** encourages children to choose healthy habits. She has a B.A. in Communication Studies and M.Ed in Education and Holistic Nutrition.

Visit Yvelette's website and blog for tips on wellness and writing.

www.yvelettestines.com
www.calmingcorners.com

Social
T: @YveletteStines + @CalmingCorners
IG: Yvelette.Stines + CalmingCorners

VERNON THE VEGETABLE MAN

Encourage the children in your life
to choose healthy habits.

Purchase Yvelette's Children's Book
Available on Amazon

www.ingramcontent.com/pod-product-compliance
Lightning Source LLC
Chambersburg PA
CBHW050604300426
44112CB00013B/2058